Floating

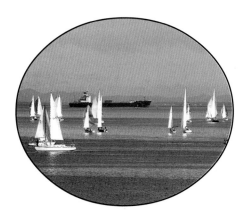

Focus: Materials

PETER SLOAN &
SHERYL SLOAN

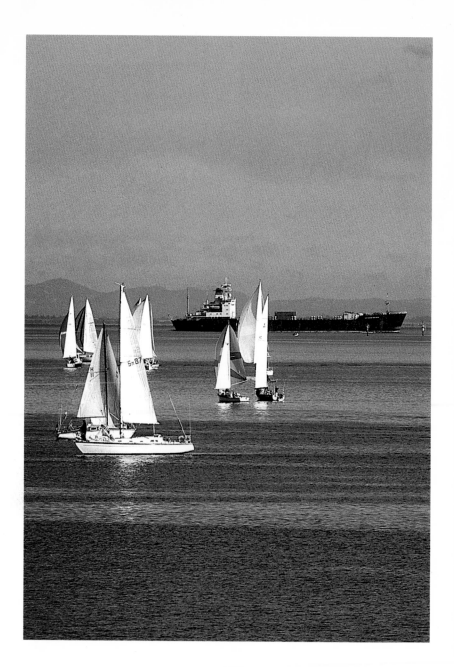

A boat can float.

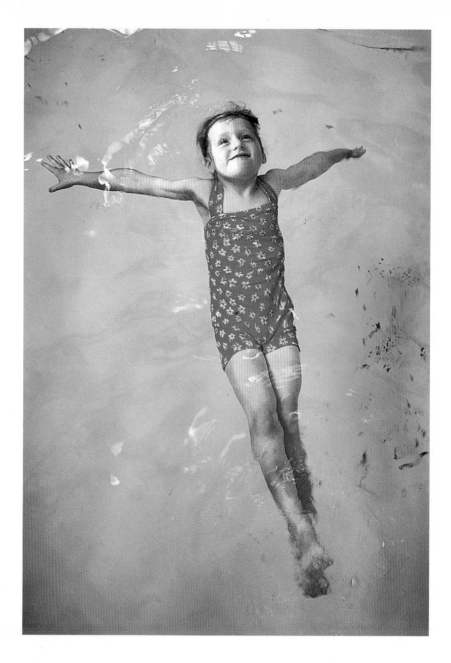

A person can float.

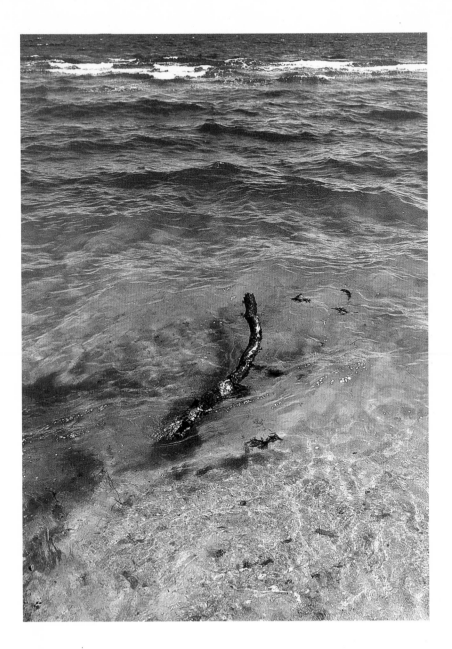

A stick can float.

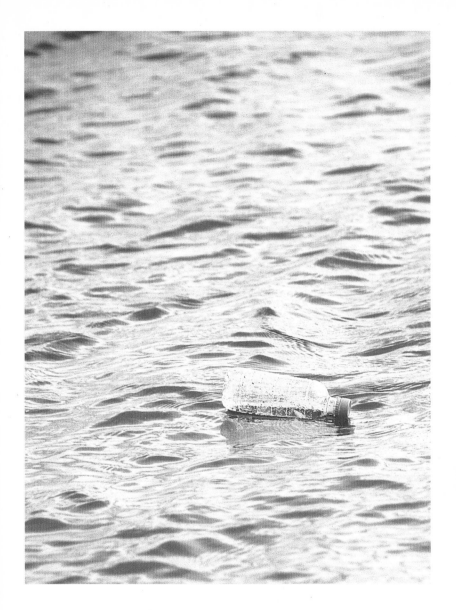

A plastic bottle
can float.

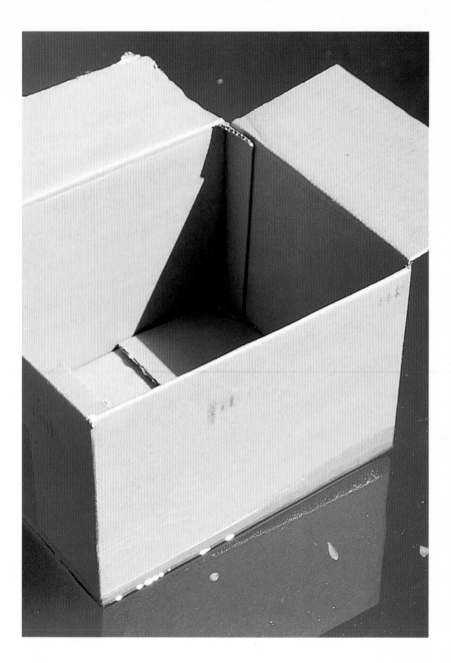

A box can float.

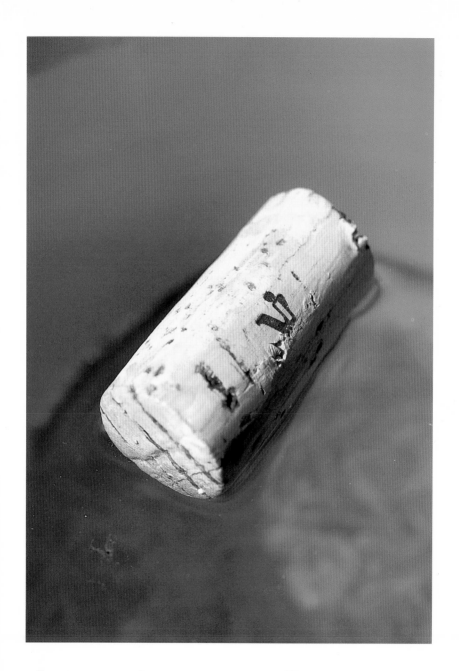

A cork can float.

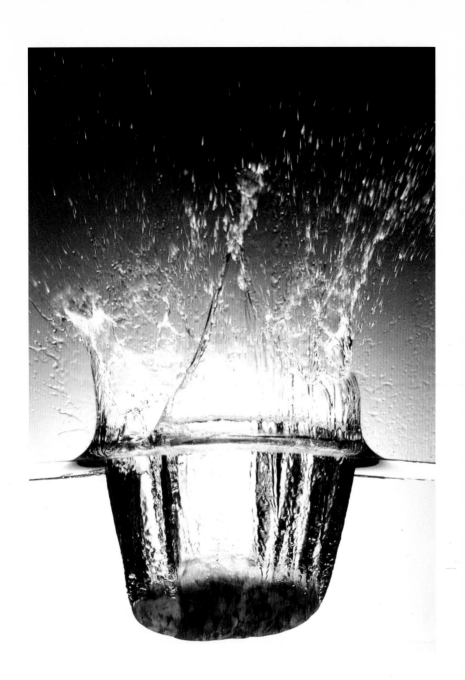

A rock will sink.